UKULELE

CHART HITS
OF 2020-2021

Front cover ukulele photo courtesy of Flight Instruments

ISBN 978-1-70513-410-8

Visit Hal Leonard Online at
www.halleonard.com

Contact us:
Hal Leonard
7777 West Bluemound Road
Milwaukee, WI 53213
Email: info@halleonard.com

In Europe, contact:
Hal Leonard Europe Limited
42 Wigmore Street
Marylebone, London, W1U 2RN
Email: info@halleonardeurope.com

In Australia, contact:
Hal Leonard Australia Pty. Ltd.
4 Lentara Court
Cheltenham, Victoria, 3192 Australia
Email: info@halleonard.com.au

CONTENTS

Afterglow

Words and Music by Ed Sheeran, David Hodges and Fred Gibson

cof - fee in your hand. My eyes are caught in your gaze ___
los - ing track of time. I'm hold - ing noth - ing a - gainst ___

___ all o - ver a - gain.
___ it 'cept you and I.

We were love ___

Chorus

___ drunk, wait - ing on a mir - a - cle, ___ tryin' to find ___

___ our - selves in the win - ter snow, so a - lone ___

___ in love like the world had dis - ap - peared. ___

Oh, I won't ___ be si - lent and I

Drivers License

Words and Music by Daniel Nigro and Olivia Rodrigo

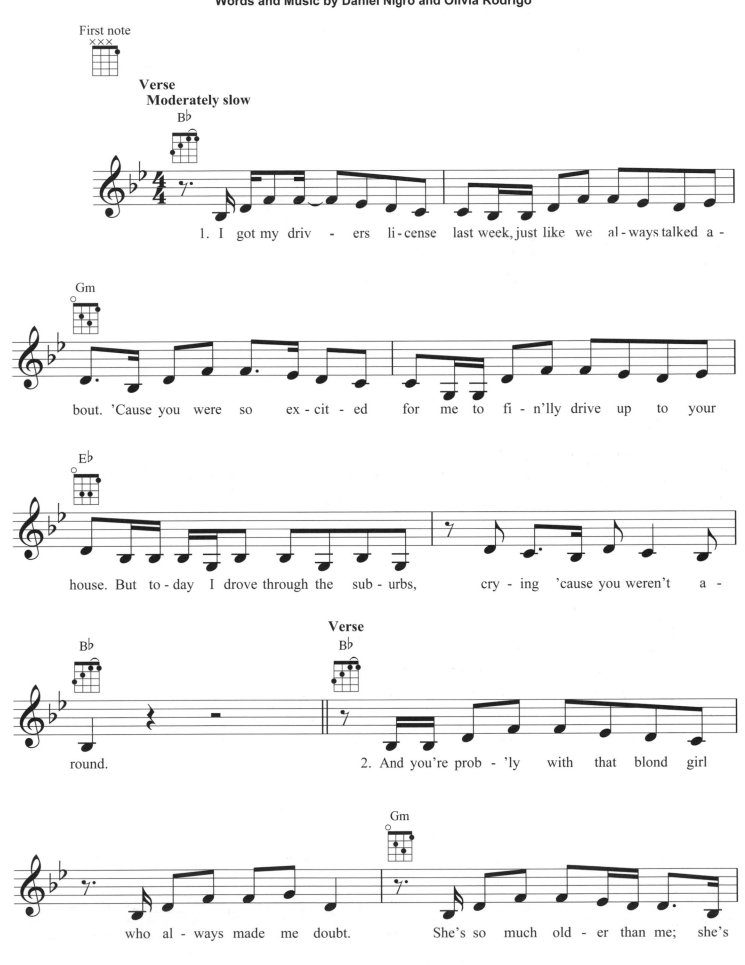

ev-'ry-thing I'm __ in - se - cure a - bout. Yeah, to - day I drove through the sub - urbs,

'cause how could I ev - er love some - one else? And

𝄋 Chorus

I know we weren't per - fect, but I've nev - er felt this way for no one. And

I just can't i - mag - ine how you could be so o - kay _____ now that I'm _

_____ gone. { Guess / I guess } you did - n't mean what you wrote in that song a - bout

me. _____   'Cause you said for-ev-er; now I drive a-lone past your

street.   3. And all my friends are tired _____

of hear-ing how much I miss you; but   I kind of feel sor-ry for them, 'cause

they'll nev-er know you the way that I do. Yeah, to-day I drove through the sub-urbs and

pic-tured I _____ was driv-ing home _____ to you. _____   And

9

no one. And I just can't i - mag - ine how you

could be so o - kay now that I'm ___ gone. Guess

you did - n't mean what you wrote in that song a - bout me. 'Cause

you said for - ev - er; now I drive a - lone past your street. Yeah,

Outro

you said for - ev - er; now I drive a - lone past your street.

Anyone

Words and Music by Justin Bieber, Jon Bellion, Jordan Johnson, Alexander Izquierdo,
Andrew Watt, Raul Cubina, Stefan Johnson and Michael Pollack

y - one. _____   If it's not _____

Oh. _____

_____ you, it's _____ not   an - y - one.   Oh, _____ yeah, _____

_____   Oh. _____

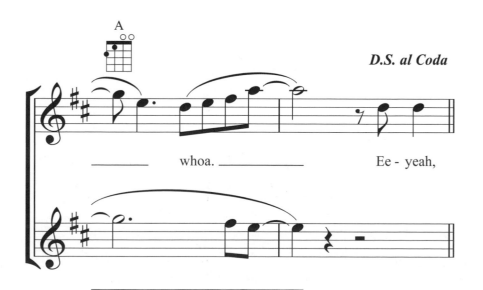

_____ whoa. _____   Ee - yeah,

y - one.

Diamonds

Words and Music by Sam Smith, Oscar Gorres and Shellback

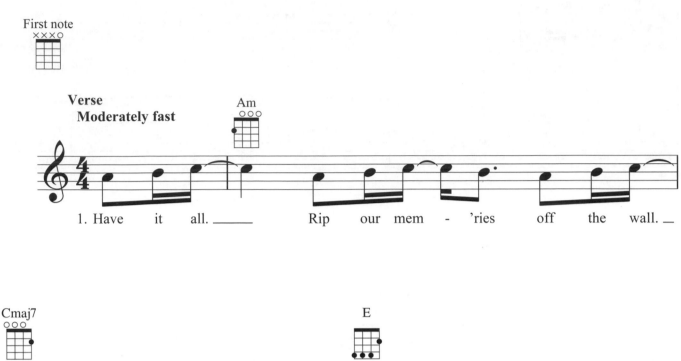

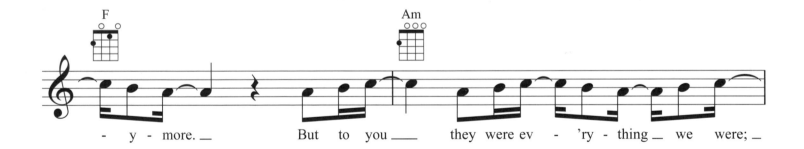

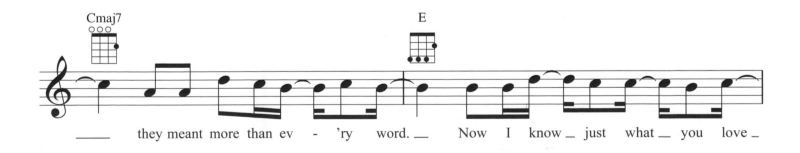

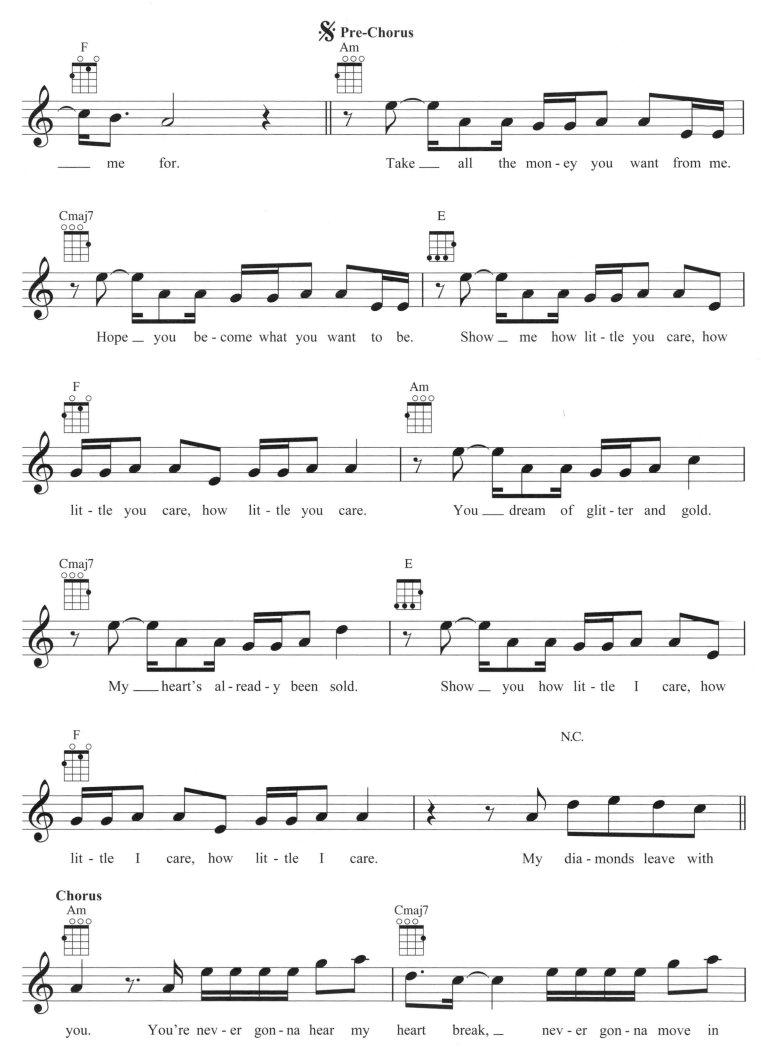

Pre-Chorus

F ___ me for.

Am Take ___ all the mon-ey you want from me.

Cmaj7 Hope ___ you be-come what you want to be.

E Show ___ me how lit-tle you care, how

F lit-tle you care, how lit-tle you care.

Am You ___ dream of glit-ter and gold.

Cmaj7 My ___ heart's al-read-y been sold.

E Show ___ you how lit-tle I care, how

F lit-tle I care, how lit-tle I care.

N.C. My dia-monds leave with

Chorus

Am you. You're nev-er gon-na hear my

Cmaj7 heart break, ___ nev-er gon-na move in

E   F

dark   ways. _   Ba - by, you're so   cruel.   My   dia - monds leave with

Am   Cmaj7

you.   Ma - te - ri - al love won't fool me. _   When you're not here I

To Coda ⊕

E   F

can breathe. _   Think I al - ways knew   my   dia - monds leave with

Verse

Am   Am

you.   2. Shake it off, ____ shake the fear _ of feel - ing lost. _

Cmaj7   E

____ Al-ways me _ that pays _ the cost. _ I should nev - er trust _ so eas -

F   Am

- i - ly. _   You lied ____ to me, _   lie, lied _

Cmaj7   E

_____ to me, _____ then left ____ with my ____ heart 'round ____ your chest. ____

F

D.S. al Coda

_____

Coda

F

knew   my   dia - monds leave with

Interlude

Am   Cmaj7

you.   Whoa,   oh, _____   whoa,   oh. ____

1.

E   F

_____   Al - ways knew   my   dia - monds leave with

2.   **Chorus**

F   Am

knew.   You're nev - er gon - na hear my

Cmaj7   E

heart break, __ nev - er gon - na move in dark ways. __ Ba - by, you're so

cruel. My dia-monds leave with you. Ma-te-ri-al love won't

fool me. __ When you're not here I can breathe. __ Think I al-ways

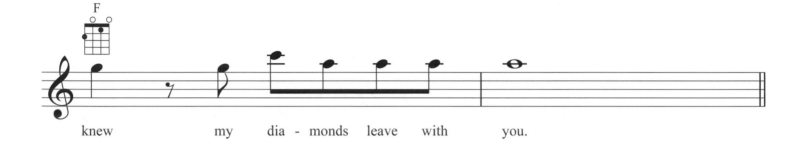

knew my dia-monds leave with you.

Chorus

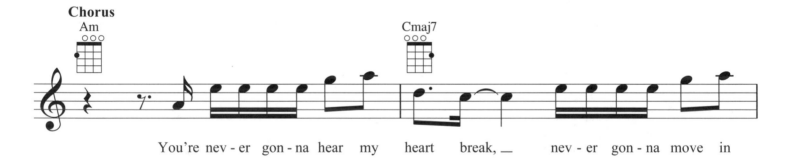

You're nev-er gon-na hear my heart break, __ nev-er gon-na move in

dark ways. __ Ba-by, you're so cruel. My dia-monds leave with

you. Ma-te-ri-al love won't fool me. __ When you're not here I

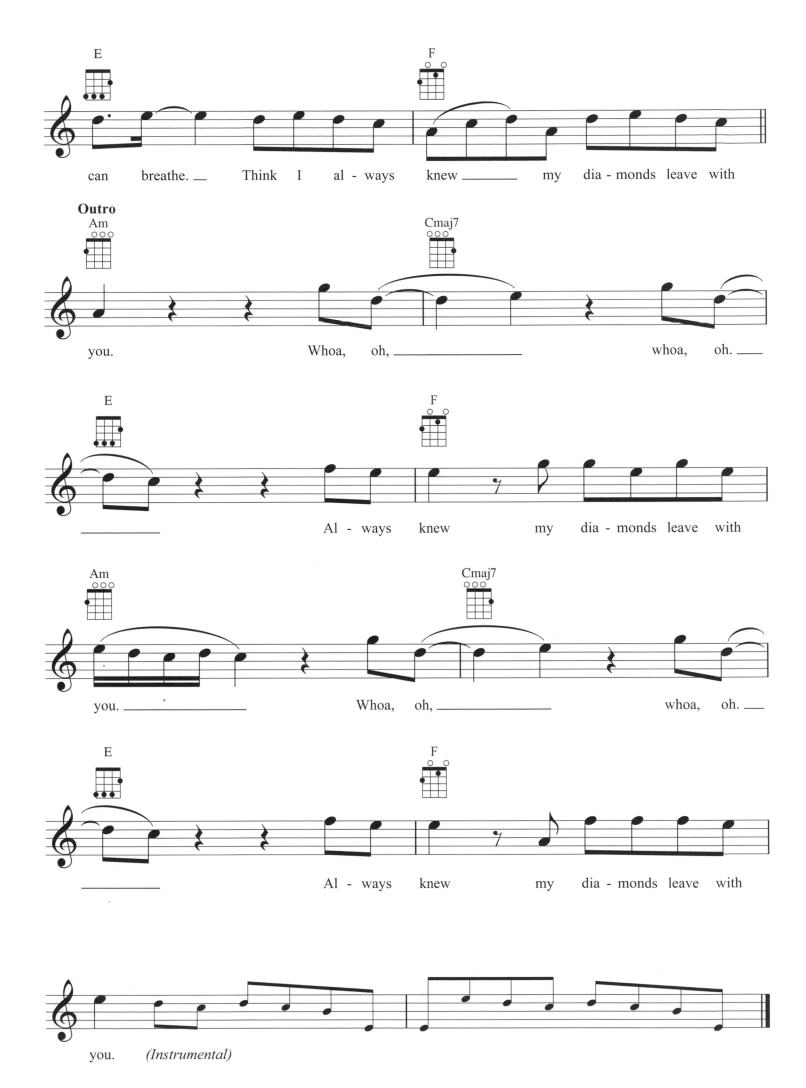

can   breathe. __   Think I   al - ways knew _____ my   dia - monds leave with

Outro

you.   Whoa,   oh, _____   whoa, oh. __

_____   Al - ways knew   my   dia - monds leave with

you. _____   Whoa,   oh, _____   whoa,   oh. __

_____   Al - ways knew   my   dia - monds leave with

you.   *(Instrumental)*

Dynamite

Words and Music by Jessica Agombar and David Stewart

Ding-dong, call me on my phone, iced tea and a game of Ping-Pong.

Pre-Chorus

This is get-ting heav-y; can you hear the bass boom?__ I'm read-y.

Life is sweet as hon-ey, yeah, this beat, cha-ching __ like mon-ey.

Dis - co o - ver-load,__ I'm in - to that,__ I'm good to go. __ I'm

dia - mond;__ you know I glow up. (Hey, so let's go!) / (Hey, let's go!) 'Cause

Chorus

I, I, I'm in the stars ___ to - night, so watch me

Light it up ____ with dy - na - mite. Dy - na - na - na - na - na - na - na, ay.

Dy - na - na - na - na - na - na - na, ay. Dy - na - na - na - na - na - na - na, ay.

Chorus

Light it up ____ with dy - na - mite. 'Cause I, I, I'm in the stars ____

____ to - night, so watch me bring the fire, set the night ____ a - light.

Shin - ing through ___ the cit - y with ___ a lit - tle funk ___ and soul. ___ So I'm a

Chorus

light it up like dy - na - mite. 'Cause I, I, I'm in the stars ___

Forever After All

Words and Music by Drew Parker, Robert Williford and Luke Combs

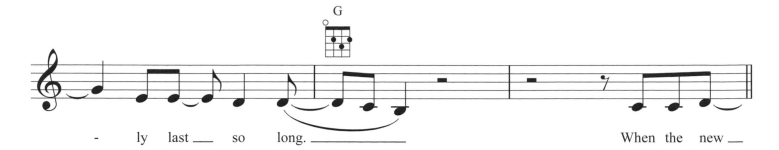

- ly last ___ so long. _____ When the new ___

Pre-Chorus

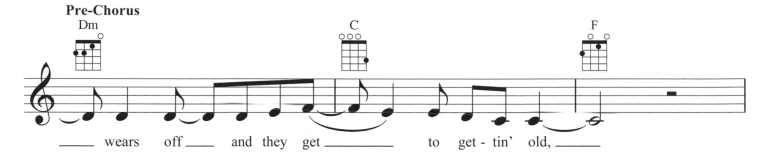

___ wears off ___ and they get _____ to get - tin' old, _____

soon - er or lat - er time's ___ gon - na take its ___ toll.

𝄋 **Chorus**

They say noth - in' lasts ___ for - ev - er, but they ain't ___

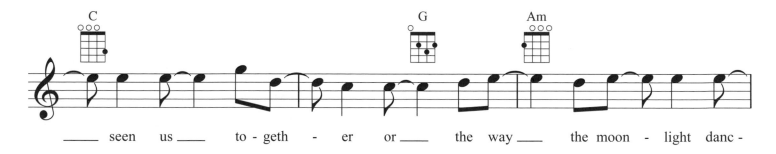

___ seen us ___ to - geth - er or ___ the way ___ the moon - light danc -

- es in ___ your eyes. _____ Just a T - shirt in ___ the kitch -

- en, with no make - up and __ a mil - lion oth - er things __

__ that I __ could look __ at my __ whole life. _____ A love __

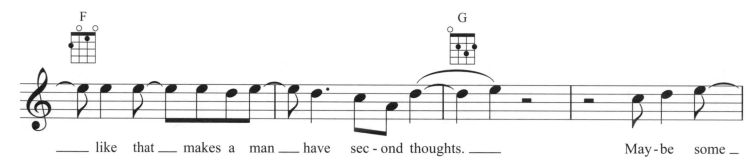

__ like that __ makes a man __ have sec - ond thoughts. ___ May - be some __

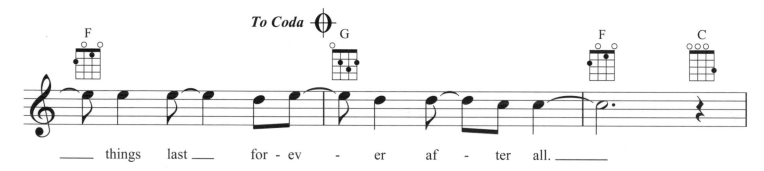

__ things last __ for - ev - er af - ter all. _____

2. F - M sta - tion on __ the out -

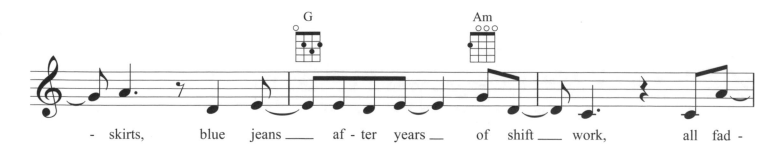

- skirts, blue jeans __ af - ter years __ of shift __ work, all fad -

- in' out ___ like I al - ways knew ___ they would. ___

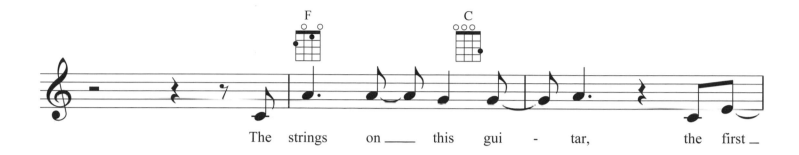

The strings on ___ this gui - tar, the first ___

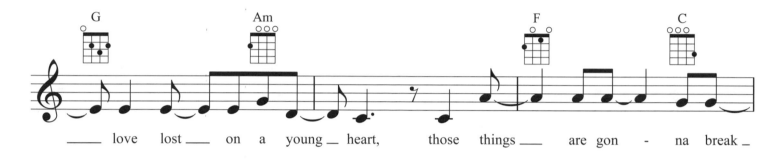

___ love lost ___ on a young ___ heart, those things ___ are gon - na break ___

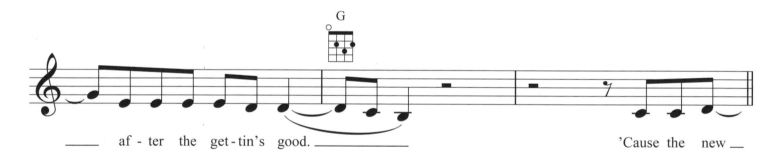

___ af - ter the get - tin's good. _____ 'Cause the new ___

Pre-Chorus

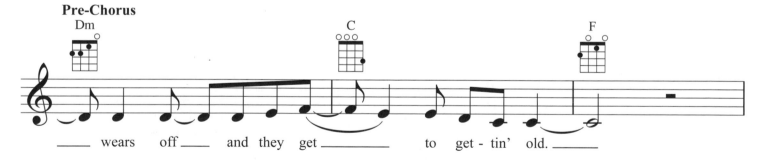

___ wears off ___ and they get _____ to get - tin' old. ___

Yeah, soon - er or lat - er time's ___ gon - na take its ___

D.S. al Coda

F G

_____ toll.   They say noth -

Coda

G

- er af - ter all. __

Interlude

Am   F   C

_____

G   **Chorus**   F

They say noth - in' lasts __ for - ev -

C   G

- er, but they ain't __ seen us __ to - geth - er or __ the way __

Am   G

_____ the moon - light danc - es in __ your eyes. _____

F

And I know __ there'll be __ that mo - ment the good Lord calls __

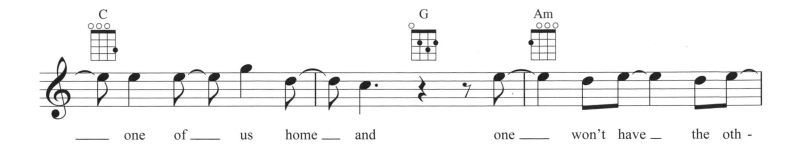

_____ one of _____ us home _____ and   one _____ won't have _____ the oth -

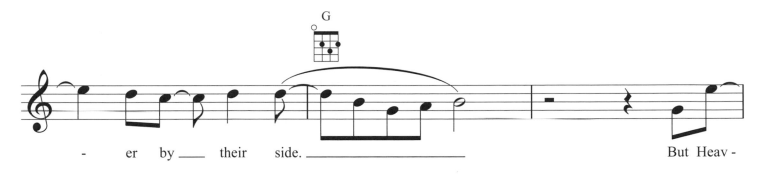

- er by _____ their side. _____   But Heav -

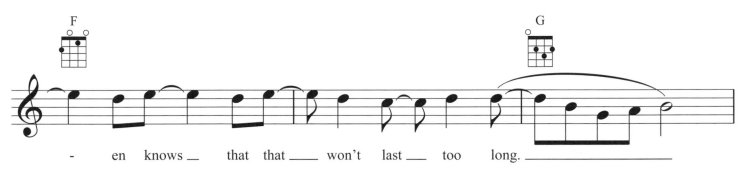

- en knows _____ that that _____ won't last _____ too long. _____

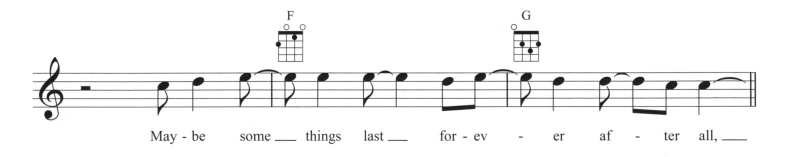

May - be some ___ things last ___ for - ev - er af - ter all, ___

Outro

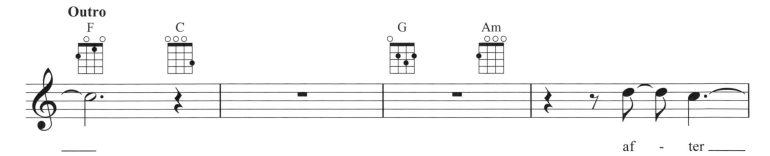

_____   af - ter _____

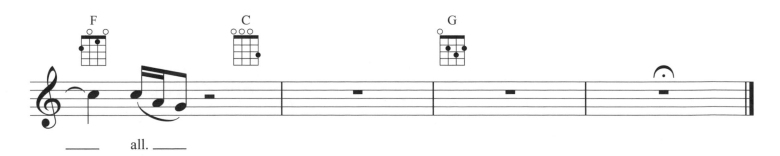

_____ all. _____

Holy

Words and Music by Justin Bieber, Jon Bellion, Anthony Jones, Tommy Brown, Steven Franks, Michael Pollack, Jorgen Odegard and Chancelor Bennett

2. | Em | C | Bridge G | D

feels so ___ ho - ly. They say we're too young and the

Em7 | C | G | D

pimps and the play-ers say, "Don't go crush-ing." Wise men say fools rush in, but

Em7 | C | G | D

I don't ___ know. ___ They say we're too young and the

Em7 | C | G | D

pimps and the play-ers say, "Don't go crush-ing." Wise men say fools rush in, but

Em7 | C | **Verse** G | D

I don't ___ know. ___ 3. The first step pleas-es the Fa -

Em | C | G | D

- ther. Might be the hard-est to take.

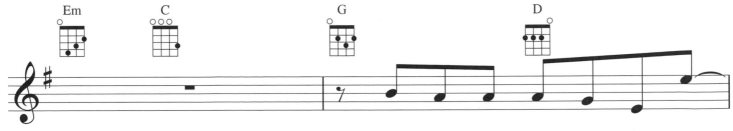

When you come out of the wa -

Rap

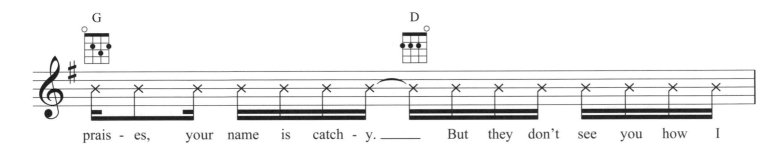

- ter, I'm a be - liev - er, my heart is flesh - y. ___ Life is short with a

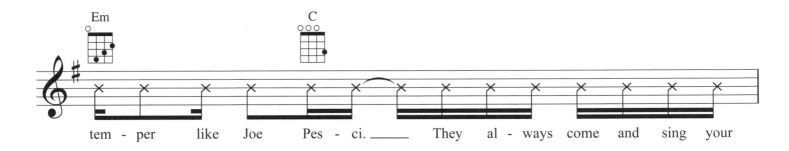

tem - per like Joe Pes - ci. _____ They al - ways come and sing your

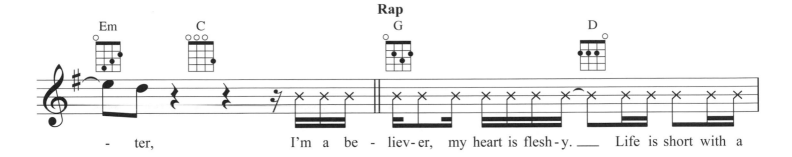

prais - es, your name is catch - y. _____ But they don't see you how I

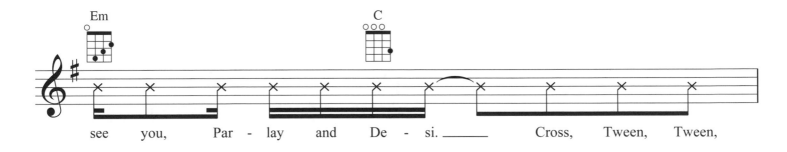

see you, Par - lay and De - si. _____ Cross, Tween, Tween,

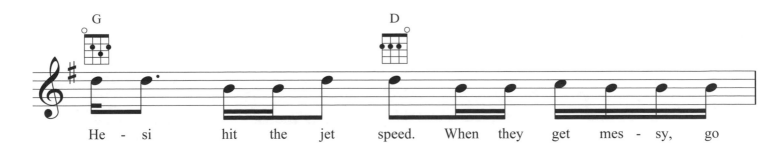

He - si hit the jet speed. When they get mes - sy, go

left - y like Lio - nel Mes - si. _____ Let's take a trip and get the

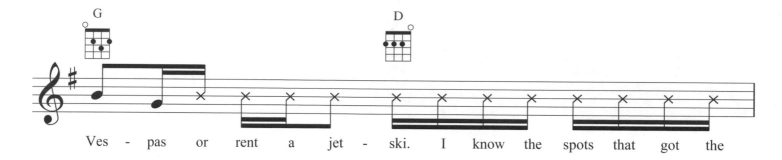

Ves - pas or rent a jet - ski. I know the spots that got the

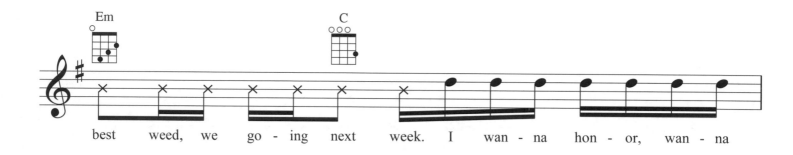

best weed, we go - ing next week. I wan - na hon - or, wan - na

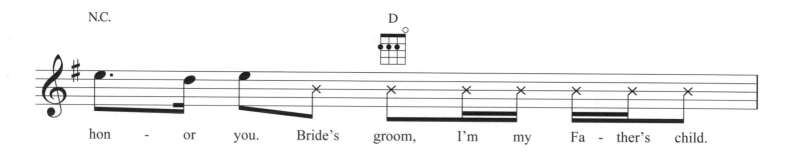

hon - or you. Bride's groom, I'm my Fa - ther's child.

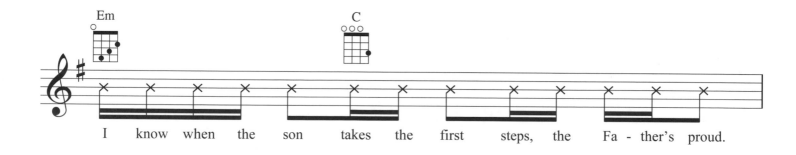

I know when the son takes the first steps, the Fa - ther's proud.

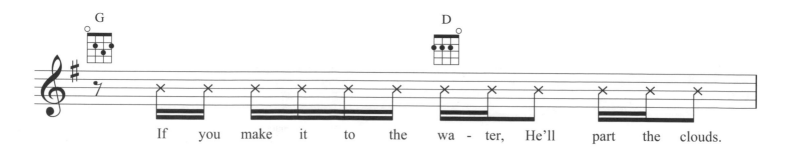

If you make it to the wa - ter, He'll part the clouds.

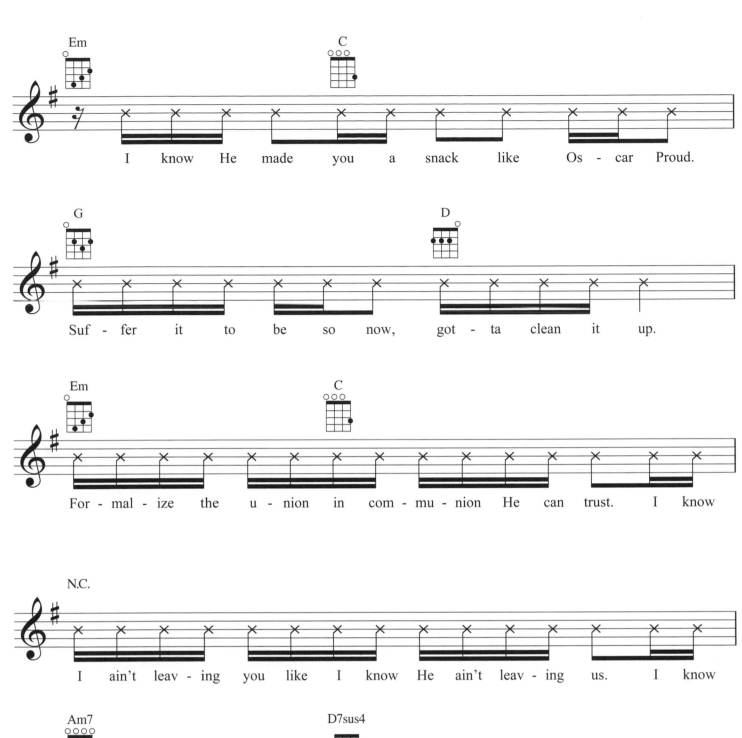

Em **C**

I know He made you a snack like Os - car Proud.

G **D**

Suf - fer it to be so now, got - ta clean it up.

Em **C**

For - mal - ize the u - nion in com - mu - nion He can trust. I know

N.C.

I ain't leav - ing you like I know He ain't leav - ing us. I know

Am7 **D7sus4**

we be - lieve in God and I know God be - lieves in us.
'Cause the way you

Pre-Chorus

G **D**

hold me, hold _____ me, hold me, hold me, hold me

feels so ho - ly, ho - ly, ho - ly, ho - ly, ho - ly.

Outro-Chorus

Oh God, run - ning to the al - tar like a track star.

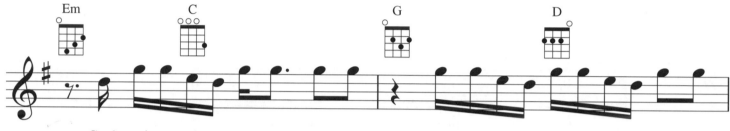

Can't wait an - oth - er sec - ond, oh God. Run - ning to the al - tar like a track star.

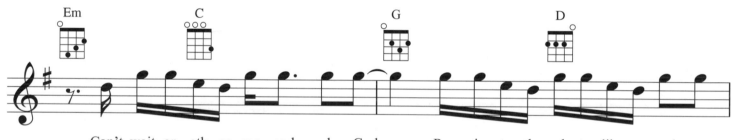

Can't wait an - oth - er sec - ond, oh God. __ Run - ning to the al - tar like a track star.

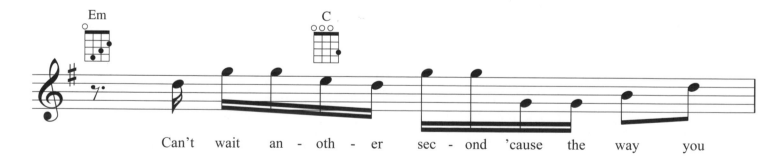

Can't wait an - oth - er sec - ond 'cause the way you

hold me, hold __ me, hold me, hold me feels so ho - ly.

Happy Anywhere

Words and Music by Ross Copperman, Josh Osborne and Matt Jenkins

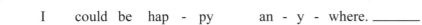

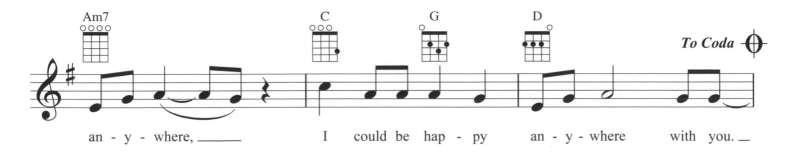

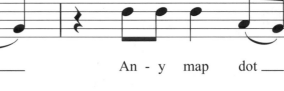

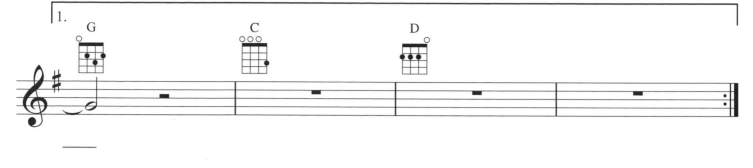

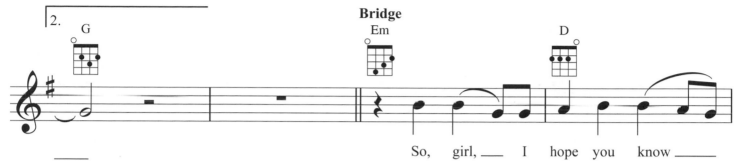

So, girl, __ I hope you know __

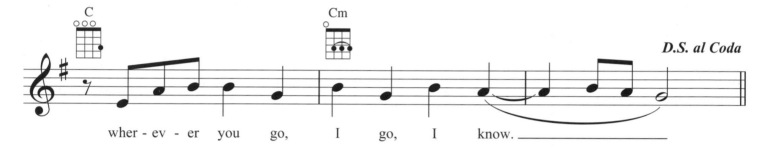

wher - ev - er you go, I go, I know. _____

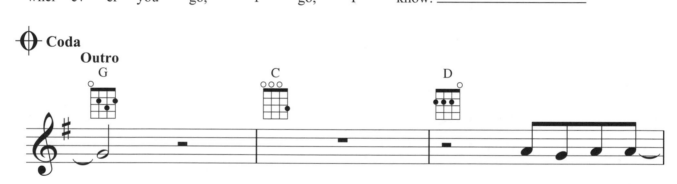

I could be hap -

- py an - y - where _____ with you. _____

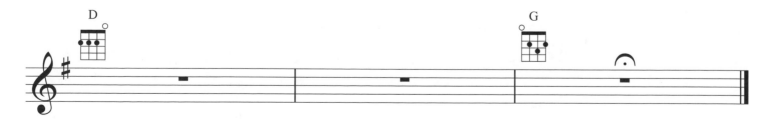

I Hope

Words and Music by Gabby Barrett, Zachary Kale and Jon Nite

Ice Cream

Words and Music by Selena Gomez, Ariana Grande, Teddy Park, Jung Hun Seo, Victoria Monét McCants, Tommy Brown, Steven Franks and Rebecca Johnson

stay on top of me so I can't see no -

bod - y else for me, no. Get it, flip it, scoop it,

do it like that, oh yeah, oh yeah. Like it, love it, lick it,

D.S. al Coda

do it like la - la - la, oh yeah.

Coda

ice cream, chill - ing.

Ice cream chill - ing, chill - ing, ice cream chill - ing.

Ice cream chill - ing, chill - ing, ice cream.

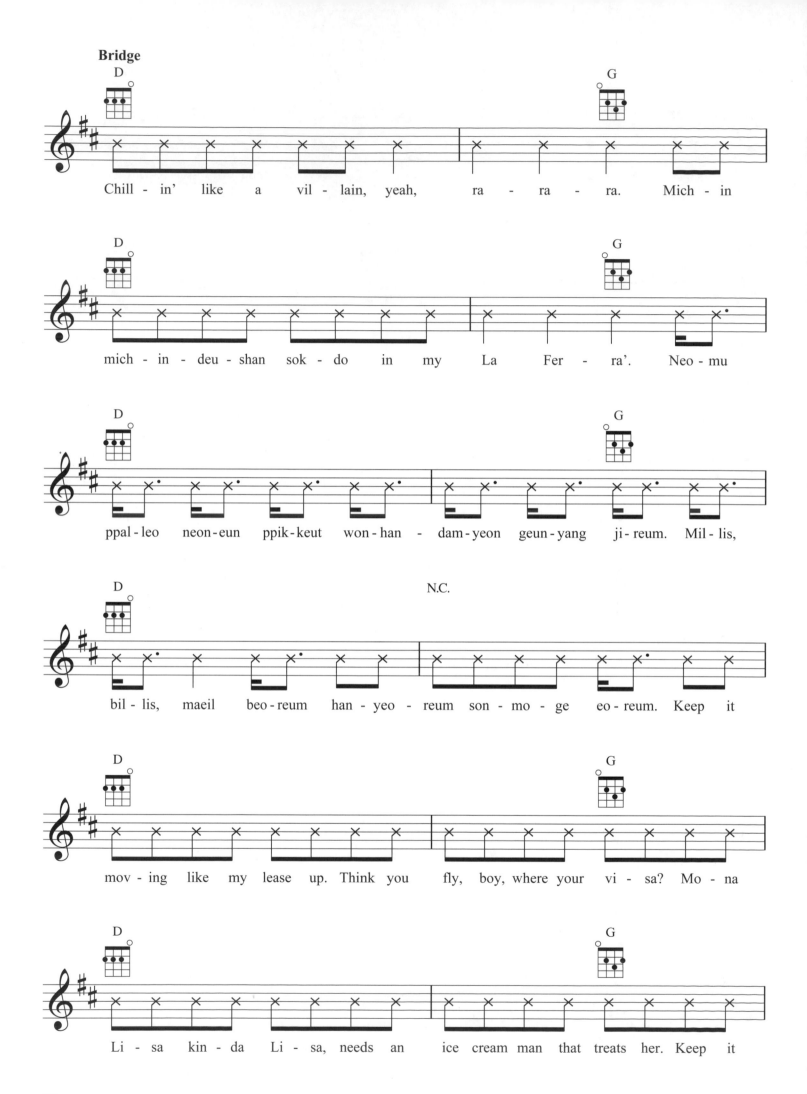

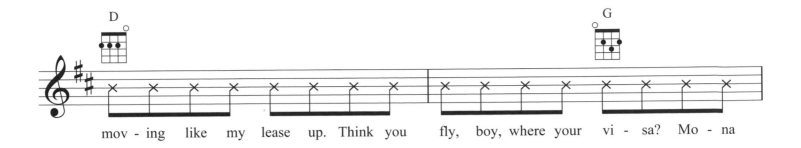

mov - ing like my lease up. Think you fly, boy, where your vi - sa? Mo - na

Li - sa kin - da Li - sa, needs an ice cream man that treats her. Hey!

Outro

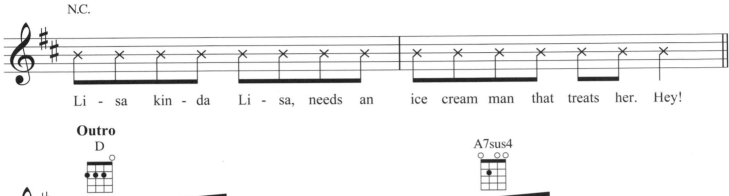

Na na na na na, na na na na na.

Ice on my wrist, yeah, I like it like this. { Get the / And I'm

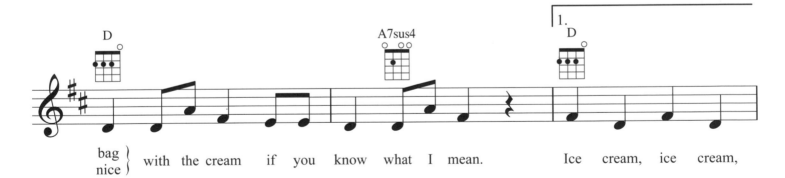

bag } / nice } with the cream if you know what I mean. Ice cream, ice cream,

ice cream chill - ing. Ice cream, ice cream, ice cream.

Monster

Words and Music by Justin Bieber, Shawn Mendes, Mustafa Ahmed, Adam Feeney and Ashton Simmonds

ev - 'ry - thing I've done.   Hold - ing   it   a - gainst   me   like

you're the ___ ho - ly one. _____   I   had   a

Pre-Chorus

chip   on   my   shoul - der,   had   to   let   it   go. _____

'cause un - for - give - ness keeps them   in   con - trol. _____   I   came

in   with   good   in - ten - tions,   then   I   let   it   go. _____

D.S. al Coda

And   now   I   real - ly   want   to   know.
What if I,   what if I

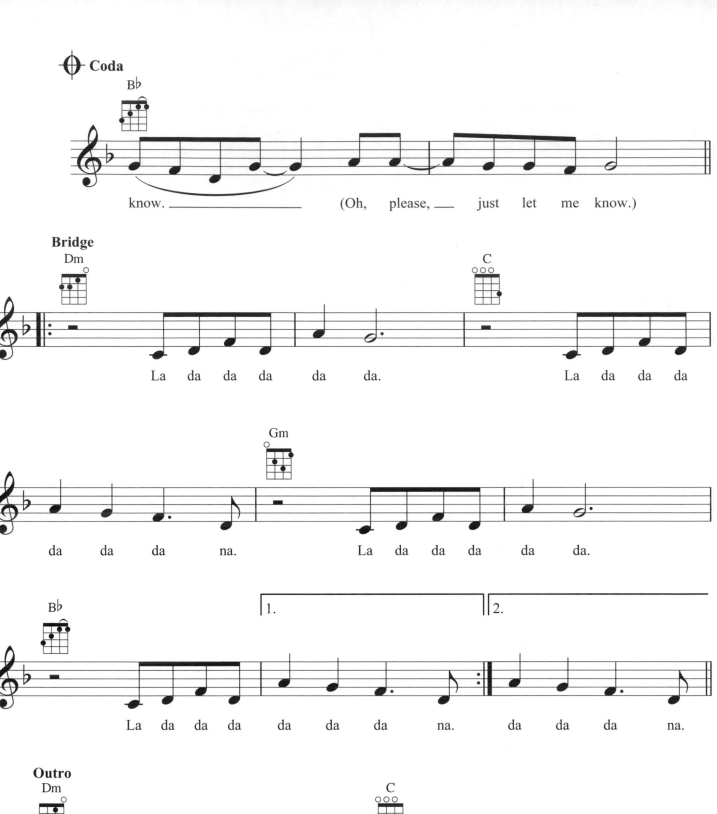

Coda

B♭

know. _____ (Oh, please, ___ just let me know.)

Bridge

Dm   C

La da da da da da.   La da da da

Gm

da da da na.   La da da da da da.

B♭   1.   2.

La da da da da da da na.   da da da na.

Outro

Dm   C

(Instrumental)

Gm   B♭

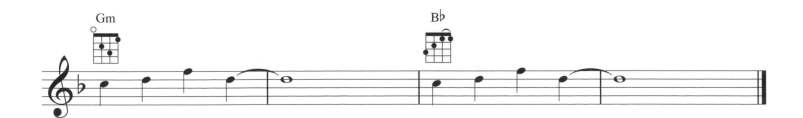

58

Kings & Queens

Words and Music by Desmond Child, Amanda Koci, Brett McLaughlin, Henry Walter, Madison Love, Mimoza Blinsson, Jakob Erixson, Nadir Khayat and Hillary Bernstein

only so much I can take. __ I'll show you how a real queen __ be-

Pre-Chorus

haves. (Oh.) _____ No dam-sel in dis-tress, don't need to save __ me. _____

_____ Once I start breath-ing fi-re, you can't tame __ me. _____

{ And you might think I'm weak with-out a sword; _____
{ And you might think I'm weak, but that is so wrong. __

_____ but if I had one, it'd be big-ger than yours. ___ }
_____ But I'm strong-er than I ev-er was _____ be-fore. __ } If

⊕ Coda   **Bridge**

Am   Dm   E♭

on your __ own. __   In chess, the king can move one

B♭   F   C

space at a time, __   but queens are free to go wher - ev - er they __ like. _____

E♭   B♭   F

You get too close, you'll get a roy - al - ty high, __   so breathe it in to feel the

A   **Chorus**
                                             Dm   Gm

love. _____   If   all of the kings __ had their

C   F   B♭   Gm

queens on the throne, __ we would pop cham - pagne __ and

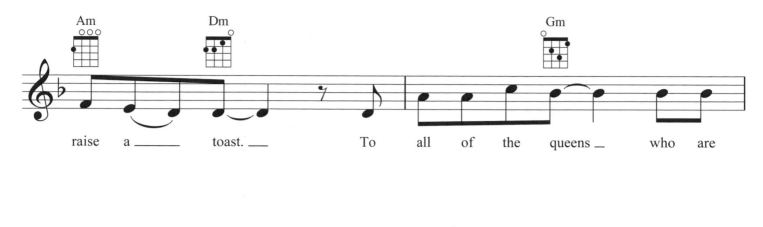

raise a _____ toast. ____ To all of the queens _____ who are

fight - ing a - lone, _____ ba - by, you're not danc - ing

Outro

on your _____ own. _____ Oh, _____

_____ oh, _____ oh, _____ oh. _____ Oh, _____

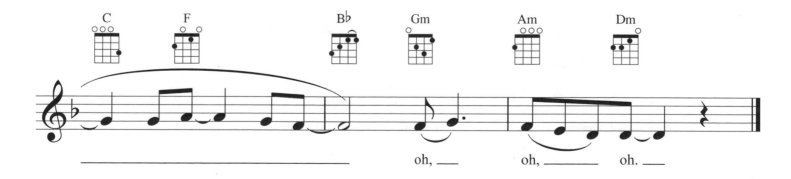

_____ oh, _____ oh, _____ oh. _____

Positions

Words and Music by Ariana Grande, Nija Charles, Tommy Brown,
Steven Franks, Angelina Barrett, Brian Bates and London Holmes

Chorus

you. Cook-ing in the kitch-en and I'm in the bed - room. I'm in the O-

lym - pics, way I'm jump-ing through hoops. Know my love in-

fi - nite, noth-ing I would-n't __ do, that I won't __ do, switch-ing for __

Outro

do, switch-ing for __ you. _____ Yeah. __

Mm, ah, _____ yeah. Ah, _____

_____ yeah. __

Starting Over

Words and Music by Chris Stapleton and Mike Henderson

jump in the wa-ter and see ____ what floats.
hard roads ____ are ____ the ones ____ worth choos - in'.

We've been sav - in' for a rain - y day. _____ Let's beat ____
Some - day we'll look ____ back and smile, _____ and know ____

____ the storm ____ and be on our way.⎫
____ it was ____ worth ____ ev - 'ry mile.⎭

And

Chorus

it don't mat-ter to me; ____ wher-ev- er we are ____ is where I ____ wan - na be. And,

hon - ey, for once ____ in our life, let's take our chanc - es and roll ____ the dice. ____

I can be your luck - y pen - ny, you can be ____ my four - leaf

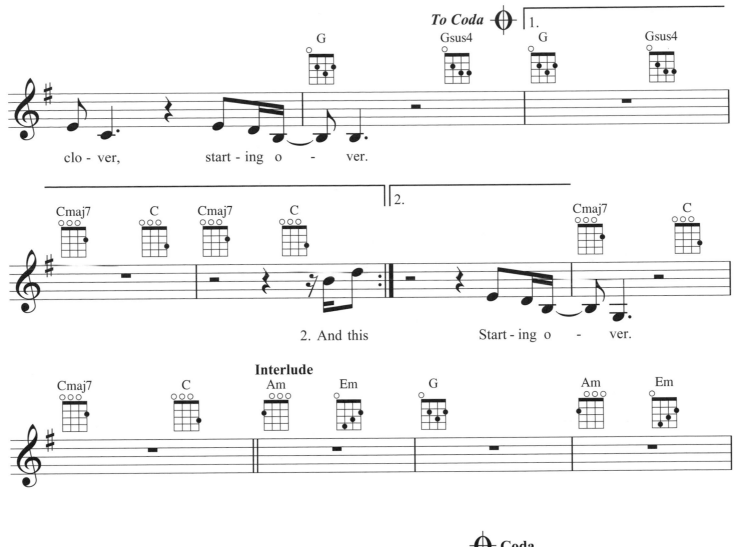

clo - ver,   start - ing o - ver.

2. And this   Start - ing o - ver.

Interlude

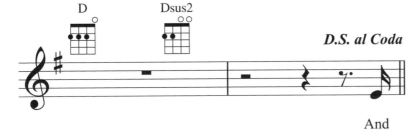

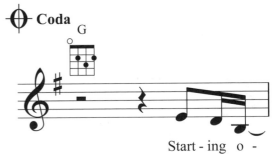

D.S. al Coda

And

Coda

Start - ing o -

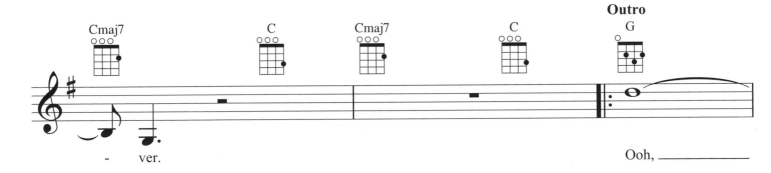

- ver.   Ooh, _____

Outro

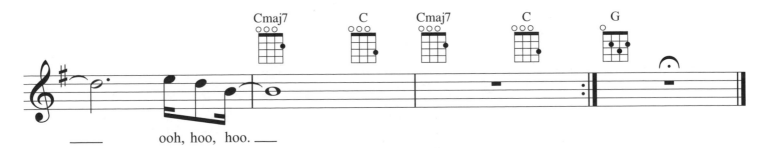

_____ ooh, hoo, hoo. _____

Prisoner

Words and Music by Miley Cyrus, Dua Lipa, Jon Bellion, Jordan Johnson, Marcus Lomax, Andrew Watt, Stefan Johnson, Ali Tamposi and Michael Pollack

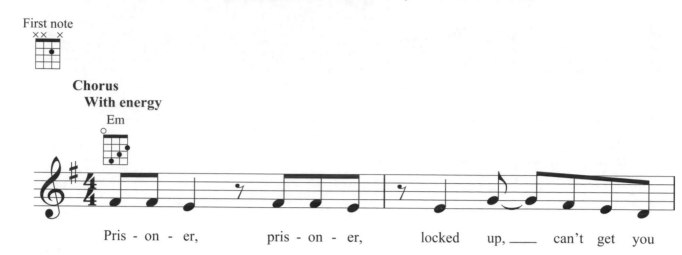

Verse

1. Strung out on a feel - ing, my hands are tied. Your face on my ceil -

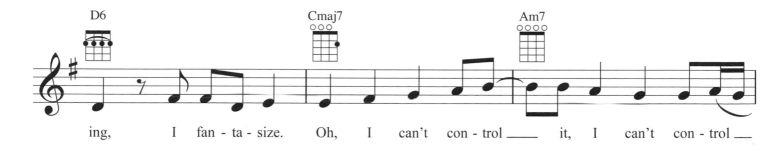

ing, I fan - ta - size. Oh, I can't con - trol ___ it, I can't con - trol ___

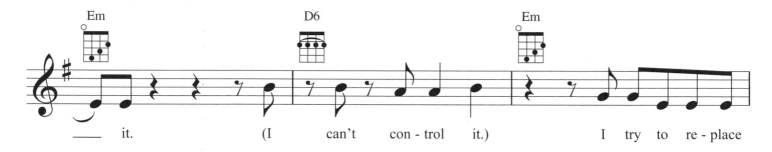

___ it. (I can't con - trol it.) I try to re - place

it with cit - y lights. I'll nev - er es - cape it, I need the high.

Oh, I can't con - trol ___ it, I can't con - trol ___ it. Oh. ___

Pre-Chorus

___ You keep mak - ing it hard - er to stay, ___ but I still ___

___ can't _ run __ a - way. __ I got - ta know: why __ can't _ you, why can't ___

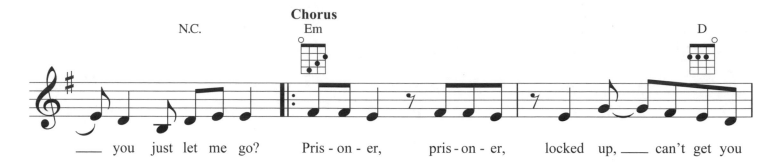

Chorus

___ you just let me go? Pris - on - er, pris - on - er, locked up, __ can't get you_

_off my mind, __ off my mind. __ Lord knows, __ I tried a_

To Coda $\oplus$

_mil - lion times, __ mil - lion times. __ Oh, __ oh, why __ can't _ you, why can't ___

1., 3.   **2.**   **Verse**

___ you just let me go?   __ you just let me go?   2. I tast - ed heav - en, now I_

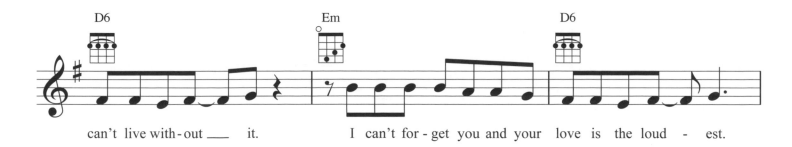

_can't live with - out __ it.   I can't for - get you and your love is the loud - est._

74

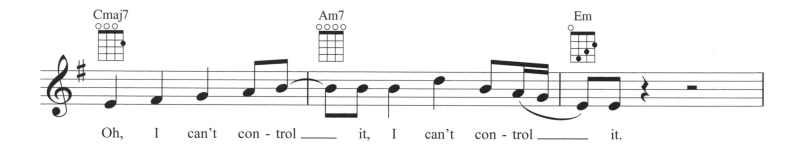

Oh, I can't con-trol _____ it, I can't con-trol _____ it.

D.S. al Coda
(with repeat)

You keep mak - ing it

Coda

_____ you just let me go?

Outro

Can't _ get you off my mind. _____ Why can't _

_____ you just let me _ go? _____ Mil - lion _____ times. I wan - na know: why _

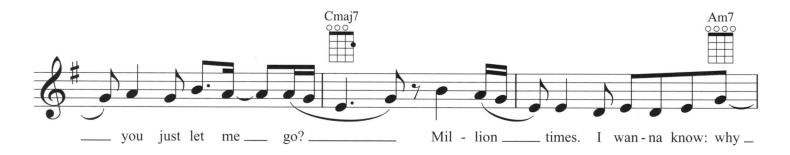

_____ can't _ you, why can't _ you? I wan - na know: why _____ can't _ you, why can't _

_____ you? I got - ta know: why _____ can't you, why can't _____ you just let me go? _____

Savage Love

Words and Music by Jason Desrouleaux, Joshua Nanai, Jacob Kasher Hindlin and Philippe Greiss

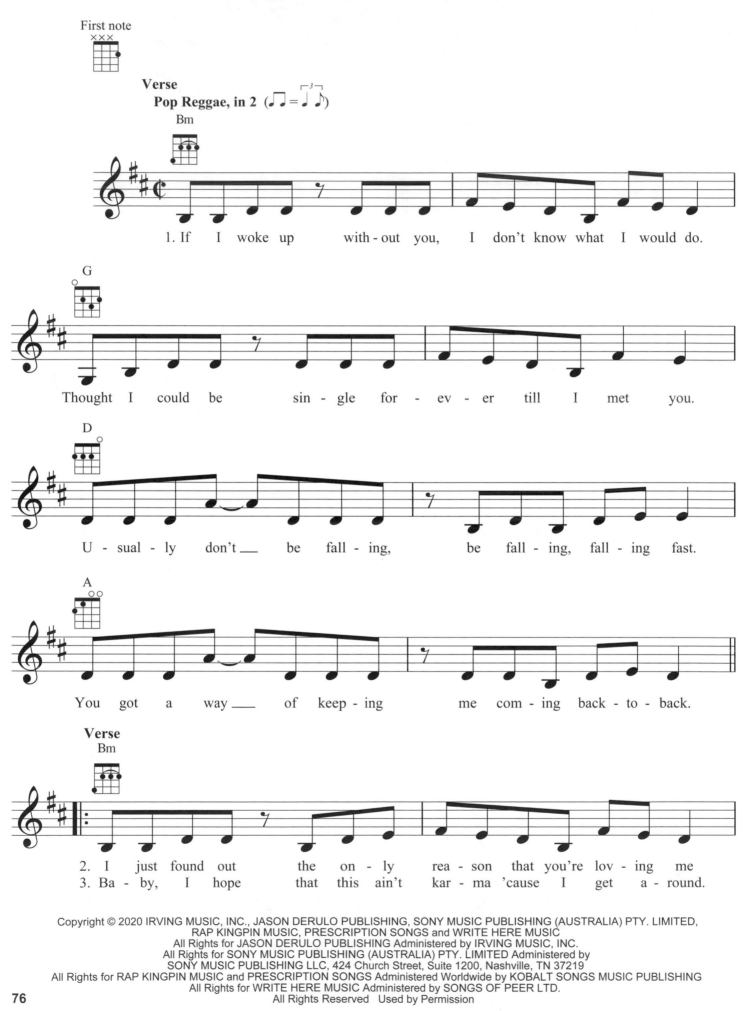

1. If I woke up with-out you, I don't know what I would do.

Thought I could be sin-gle for-ev-er till I met you.

U-sual-ly don't __ be fall-ing, be fall-ing, fall-ing fast.

You got a way __ of keep-ing me com-ing back-to-back.

2. I just found out the on-ly rea-son that you're lov-ing me.
3. Ba-by, I hope that this ain't kar-ma 'cause I get a-round.

was to get back at your ex - lov - er, but be - fore you leave;
You wan - na run it up, I wan - na lock it down.

u - sual - ly I _____ would nev - er, would nev - er e - ven care.
U - sual - ly don't __ be fall - ing, be fall - ing, fall - ing fast.

Ba - by, I know __ she creep - ing, I feel it in the air.
You got a way __ of mak - ing me spend up all my cash.

Pre-Chorus

Ev - 'ry night and ev - 'ry day, _____

I try _____

to make you stay, but _____ your... _____

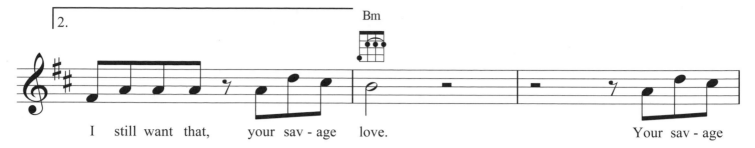

2. I still want that, your sav-age love. Your sav-age

G
lo - lo - love. _____ Your sav-age

D
lo - lo - love. _____ You could use _____ me. _____

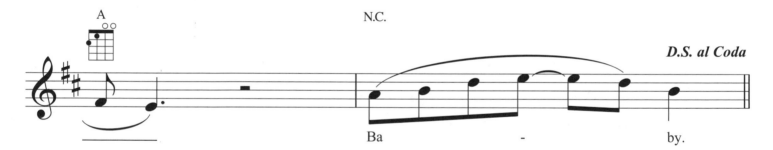

A   N.C.   *D.S. al Coda*
_____   Ba -   by.

 Coda
D
Girl, you could use _____ me _____ 'cause

A   N.C.(Bm)
I still want that, your sav-age love.

Therefore I Am

Words and Music by Billie Eilish O'Connell and Finneas O'Connell

talk 'bout me like how you might know how I feel. ____ Top of the world, _ but your world is-n't real. _

____ Your world's an i - deal. ___ So, go have

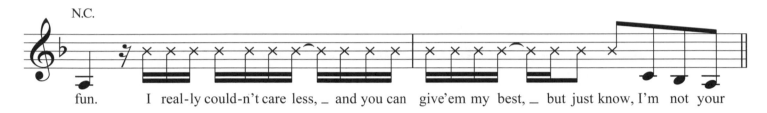

fun. I real-ly could-n't care less, _ and you can give'em my best, _ but just know, I'm not your

𝄋 Chorus

friend, or an - y - thing. Damn, you think that you're the

man. _ I think, there-fore I am. _ I'm not your friend, or an - y - thing.

To Coda ⊕

Damn, you think that you're the man. _ I think, there-fore I am. _

Verse

2. I don't want press to put ___ your name next to mine. ___ We're on dif-f'rent lines, ___ so I

wan-na be nice e - nough they don't call my bluff. ___ 'Cause I hate to find ___

ar - ti - cles, ar - ti - cles, ar - ti - cles. Rath - er you re - main un - re - mark - a - ble. (Got a lot - ta)

in - ter - views, in - ter - views, in - ter - views. When they say your name, I just act con - fused. Did you have

D.S. al Coda

fun? *(Spoken:) I really couldn't care less, and you can give 'em my best, but just know,* I'm not your

⊕ Coda

A

Bridge

Dm

am. ___ I'm sor - ry, I don't think I caught your

82

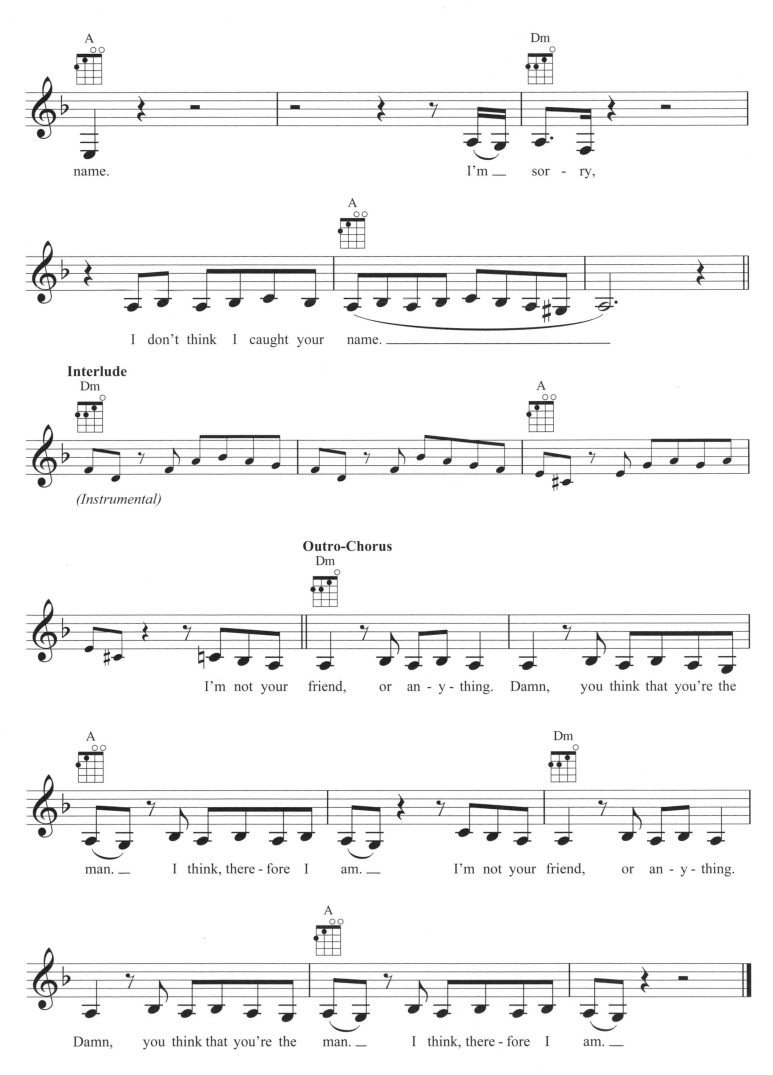

Watermelon Sugar

Words and Music by Harry Styles, Thomas Hull, Mitchell Rowland and Tyler Johnson

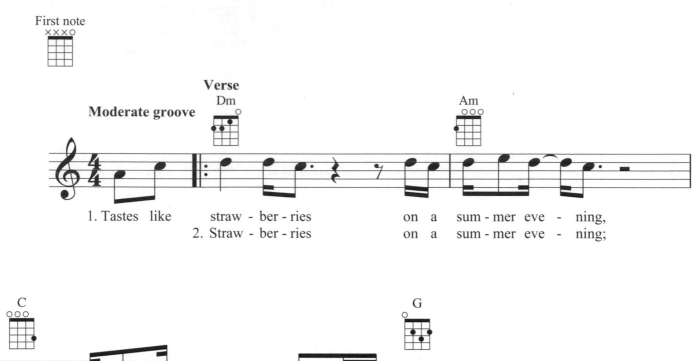

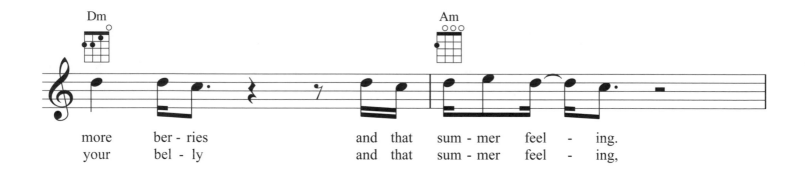

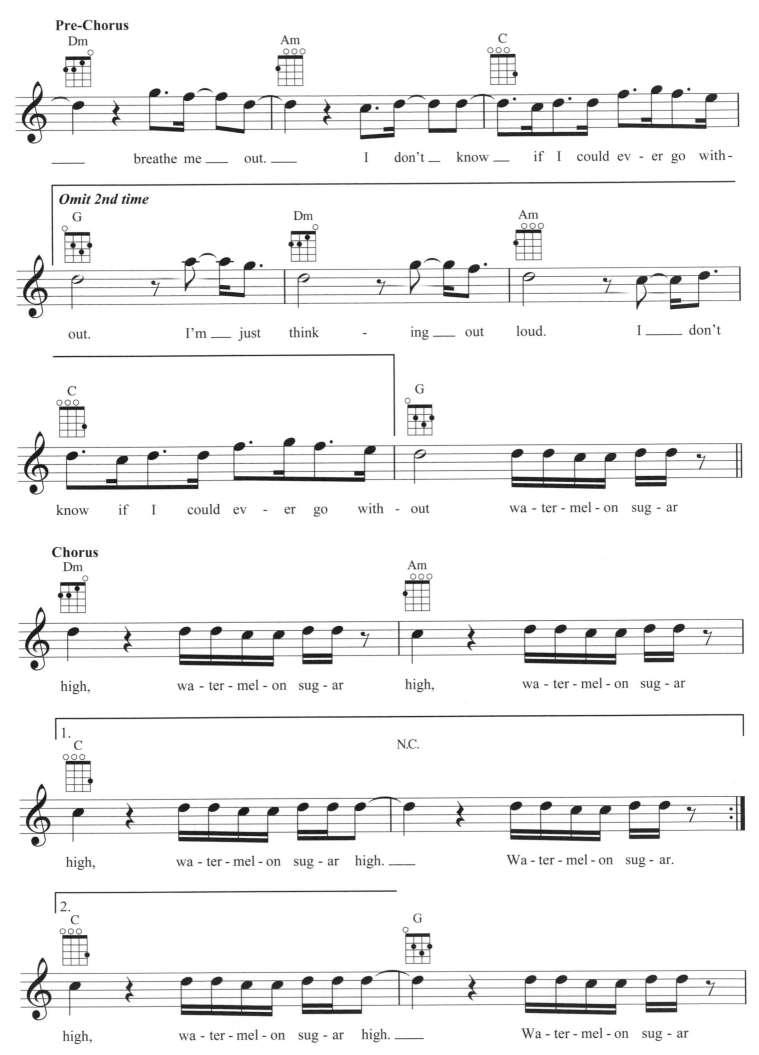

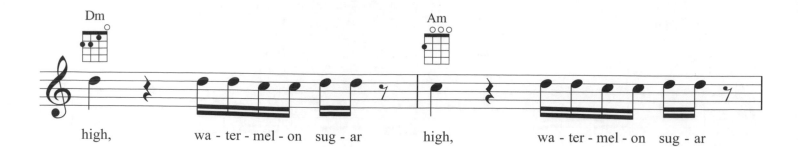

high, wa - ter - mel - on sug - ar high, wa - ter - mel - on sug - ar

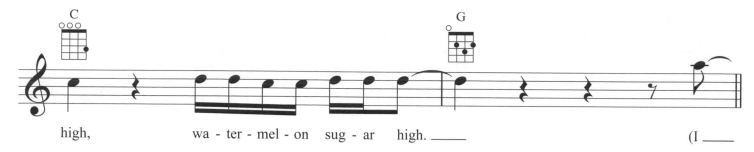

high, wa - ter - mel - on sug - ar high. ____ (I ____

Bridge

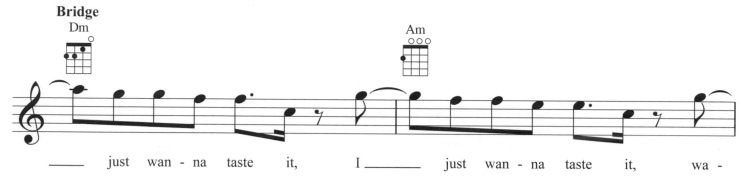

____ just wan - na taste it, I ____ just wan - na taste it, wa -

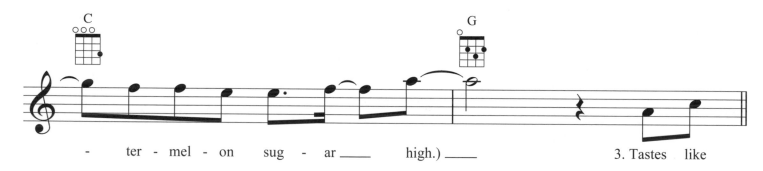

- ter - mel - on sug - ar ____ high.) ____ 3. Tastes like

Verse

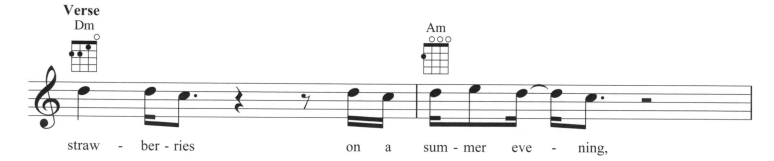

straw - ber - ries on a sum - mer eve - ning,

and it sounds _ just like a song. __ I want your bel - ly and that

sum - mer feel - ing. I _____ don't know if I could ev - er go with -

Chorus

out wa - ter - mel - on sug - ar high, wa - ter - mel - on sug - ar

high, wa - ter - mel - on sug - ar high, wa - ter - mel - on sug - ar high. _____

1.
_____ Wa - ter - mel - on sug - ar _____ I _____

2.

Outro

_____ just wan - na taste it, I _____ just wan - na taste it, wa - ter - mel - on sug - ar _____ high. _____

1.

2.

_____ I _____ - ter - mel - on sug - ar high. _____ Wa - ter - mel - on sug - ar.

You Broke Me First

Words and Music by Tate McRae, Blake Harnage and Victoria Zaro

1. May-be you don't like talk-ing too much a - bout your - self, __ but

you should-'ve told me that you were think-ing 'bout some - one __ else. __ You're

drunk at a par - ty, or may-be it's just that your car broke __ down. __ Your

phone has been off for a cou-ple months; you're call - ing me __ now. __

I know you; you're like this. When shit don't go your way, you need - ed

me to fix it. _____ And like me, I did. But

Chorus

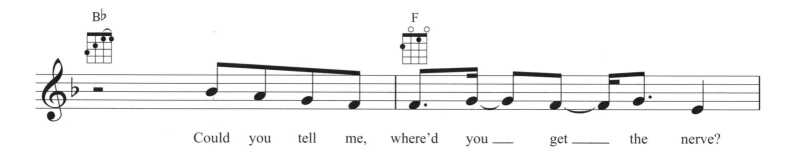

I ran out of ev-'ry rea - son. Now sud-den-ly you're ask-ing __ for __ it back.

Could you tell me, where'd you __ get _____ the nerve?

Yeah, you could say you miss all ___ that ___ we had,

but I don't real-ly care how __ bad __ it hurts when you broke me

To Coda ⊕

first. You broke me first.

Willow

Words and Music by Taylor Swift and Aaron Dessner

train could take you home; an-y-where else is hol -

low. I'm beg-ging for you to take my hand, wreck my

plans. That's my man.

Bridge

Life was a wil-low and it bent right to your

1.

wind. ___ They count ___ me out

time and time a-gain.

Outro